My Pink Piggy Bank

Here is my piggy bank.
Round and pink.

CLINK
CLINK
CLINK

I put in my coins.
"Clink, clink, clink!"

I put in five pennies.
I put in a dime.

I put in two nickels,
one at a time.

I put in a quarter
and a 50-cent piece.

ICE CREAM
1 SCOOP
25¢
2 SCOOPS
50¢

I use my coins
for a little treat.

My coins add up.
I jump. I holler.

Now my coins
will make a dollar!

Here is my piggy bank.
Round and pink.

I put in my coins.
"Clink, clink, clink!"